MAY / WALSH

Misty / *Kerri*

Dynamic Duo

MAY / WALSH
Misty / *Kerri*
Dynamic Duo

BY Ellen **Aim**

SPORT STARS

Creative media Publishing

CREATIVE MEDIA, INC.
PO Box 6270
Whittier, California 90609-6270
United States of America

www.CREATIVEMEDIA.net

Edited by Christine Dzidrums
Book & cover design by Joseph Dzidrums
Cover Photo by Scott Alan / PR Photos

First Edition: August 2016

LCCN: On File

ISBN: 978-1-938438-93-6
eISBN: 978-1-938438-94-3

Table of Contents

"From day one we just had a synergy about us."
- Kerri

The legendary, basketball star Michael Jordan once said, "Talent wins games, but teamwork and intelligence wins championships."

That quote applies perfectly to Misty May-Treanor and Kerri Walsh Jennings, the greatest beach volleyball team of all time. Winners of three straight Olympic gold medals (2004, 2008, and 2012), the dynamic duo are tremendous role models whose stellar skills, exemplary teamwork, and incredible sportsmanship should be emulated by all sports fans.

At the ESPY Awards
Albert L. Ortega / PR Photos

"I spent many extra hours training because I had a goal and I didn't want to short change myself."
- Misty

On July 30, 1977, Misty Elizabeth May was born in Los Angeles, California, to Barbara and Butch May. In hindsight, the baby's birthplace seemed fitting since Misty would one day become a major sports star.

Misty was named after the daughter of Butch's cousin. She had two older half-brothers, Brack and Scott, from her father's first marriage. Years later, Brack became a respected chef and was featured on The Food Network's *Chopped* series. The three May siblings developed a tight bond that remained strong through adulthood.

Misty's Olympic success seemed predestined given her athletic genes. Her mom had once been a nationally-ranked tennis player who grew to love volleyball. Meanwhile, her father grew up surfing in Hawaii and loved football with all his heart. Eventually, he discovered volleyball and played on the United States men's team at the 1968 Olympics.

In addition, Misty's aunt, Betty Ann Grubb Stuart, played tennis professionally. She reached the US Open finals in doubles with Renee Richards and competed at Wimbledon several times. Her children,

Taylor and Brett-Hansen Dent, were also successful tennis players.

A typical California girl, Misty practically grew up on Muscle Beach in Santa Monica. Her parents owned a pizza stand on the nearby pier. Whenever they found free time, they played or watched beach volleyball games.

Muscle Beach boasted a tight-knit volleyball community that served as a second family for the Mays. When Misty's parents were busy, their volleyball playing friends often cared for their young daughter.

For a while, a young man named Karch Kiraly even babysat Misty. The handsome UCLA biochemistry student also played on the college's volleyball team. An exceptional talent, Kiraly eventually won gold medals at the 1984, 1988, and 1996 Olympics. His first two wins were in indoor volleyball, while his third victory occurred in beach volleyball. Nowadays, Kiraly is widely considered America's best volleyball player ever.

Before long, baby Misty began crawling around Muscle Beach. One afternoon, the curious child decided sand looked especially yummy so she tasted it. Fortunately, it wasn't to her liking. She quickly shunned the coarse material in favor of smashed bananas and diced peaches.

At Home on the Sand
Daniel Locke / PR Photos

Constantly near a court, "ball" was Misty's first word. When she began walking, she was handed her first volleyball and the rest was history.

In Misty's early years, the young girl spent most of her time on Muscle Beach. When she was old enough to play volleyball, she utilized the best coach in the business - her father. One often found the Mays playing a game with the famed Santa Monica Pier as their backdrop.

As a youngster, Misty also joined AYSO, the American Youth Soccer Organization. Because there weren't any girl teams, she played every position but goalie on a co-ed team coached by her father. A versatile athlete, the young girl competed in swim meets and tennis matches, too.

When Misty was eight years old, she entered her first volleyball tournament. She was thrilled to play her debut match with her dad as her partner. Ultimately, the team finished in fifth place and the youngest May was smitten with the sport.

Misty's fondness for volleyball increased greatly over the years. Despite her burgeoning career, her parents insisted she also pay strict attention to her studies. They knew an injury could end an athlete's career in the blink of an eye, but an education lasted a lifetime.

Playing at a Charity Event
Daniel Locke / PR Photos

At age 13, Misty joined an elite indoor volleyball club called the Asics Tigers. It was one of the best teams in that age group in the country. Every team member possessed phenomenal talent.

Most of the girls on the Tigers were older than Misty. She liked it that way. The determined girl knew that playing against older players would make her a better player. In the end, the youngest Tiger helped them finish second at the Junior Olympics.

During Misty's early teen years, the Mays moved from Santa Monica to Costa Mesa, California, in Orange County. Butch began working as a film technician, while Barbara became a florist.

Misty attended Newport Harbor High School. An exceptional athlete, she participated in many extracurricular activities, like tennis, soccer, and the dance team. To this day, the well-rounded athlete believes that a person benefits physically and emotionally from playing multiple sports.

The outgoing teenager also ran on the track and field team. At the CIF California State Meet, she placed second in the high jump behind future heptathlete Tracye Lawyer. In her first year competing, she high-jumped 5-3.

Not surprisingly, Misty also played on Newport Harbor High's indoor volleyball team. The talented player led her school's team to state championships in 1992 and 1994. The exceptional athlete also earned 1993 Division I All-CIF Team Player of the Year honors, and in 1994, *USA Today* declared her the nation's best girls' volleyball player.

In 1994, Misty began attending Long Beach State. As the captain of the 49ers girls' volleyball team, she led the team to an undefeated 1998 season. The California native collected many Big West Conference honors, NCAA accolades, and back-to-back Player of the Year victories.

When graduation beckoned, Misty ended her volleyball career as one of college's most dominant players ever. There was only one level left for the volleyball phenom to conquer: the professionals!

Legendary Pair
Daniel Locke / PR Photos

"It's important to be a role model."
- Misty

In the summer of 1999, Misty joined the U.S. Women's National Volleyball Team and moved to Colorado to train in the Centennial State. She had high expectations from the start. Some people called her the savior of women's indoor volleyball, while others proclaimed that she would become the Mia Hamm of volleyball.

Shortly after joining the team, Misty's heart felt heavy. Indoor volleyball no longer felt fun anymore. The 22-year-old longed to play beach volleyball.

In late July, the U.S. women's volleyball team flew to Winnipeg, Canada, to compete in the Pan American Games. Although the United States scored a bronze medal, Misty was distracted throughout the competition. The phenomenal talent felt envious of the beach volleyball athletes and could not take her eyes off them.

"I kept thinking I should be out there on the sand," she later told the *Los Angeles Times*.

After much deliberation, Misty quit indoor volleyball and began pursuing her passion, beach volleyball. Right off the bat, she found a stellar partner in Holly McPeak, a three-time Olympian. They played their first tournament in November of 1999. Seeded 22nd, the new team finished in ninth place in their first game.

Throughout the year, the team steadily climbed up the rankings. Although they began the season as long shots to make the Olympic team, they quickly became favorites.

Meanwhile, Misty had zero qualms about changing to beach volleyball. She felt thrilled that she could roam freely on the court and wasn't limited to one role anymore.

"I love it," she told the *Los Angeles Times*. "I love the scramble plays. I love playing defense.

"Indoor, there are certain plays. Beach, it's never the same play twice."

Around the same time, Misty's mother, who had been suffering from back pain for two years, discovered she had cancer that had metastasized from her lungs to her spine to her hip to the base of her skull. Although Misty wanted to move back home to care for her mother, her parents insisted she pursue her dream.

ᴮʏEllen**Aim**

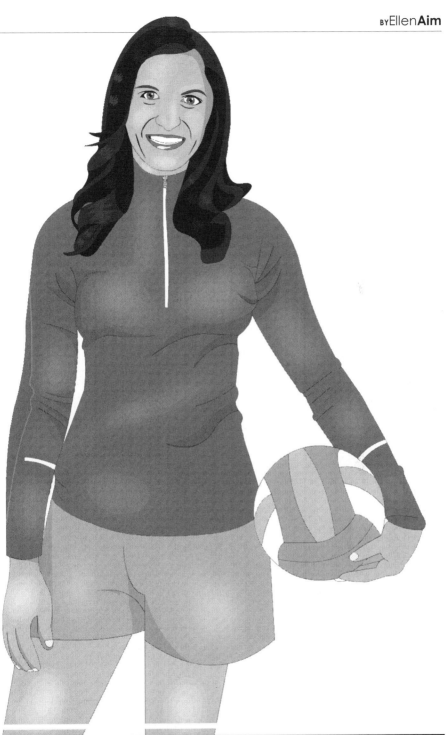

Illustration of Misty

Despite pairing later than their competitors, the duo quickly assembled a strong resume. They won their first tournament in April 2000 and followed their inaugural victory with several more wins. During their entire rookie season, they never finished lower than fifth in any tournament.

The duo felt ecstatic when they qualified for a berth at the 2000 Sydney Olympics. Although an abdominal injury hindered Misty in Australia, the American team still managed an impressive fifth place after less than a year together. More importantly, the Olympian was elated that her mom had felt well enough to attend the games and watch her compete.

Sadly, two years later, Barbara lost her battle with cancer. After her mother's death, Misty got a new tattoo of an angel with the initials BM.

Following the Sydney Olympics, Misty and Holly ended their partnership. Although Misty greatly admired the legendary player, she wanted a partner with whom she could grow as an athlete.

Luckily, another top player named Kerri Walsh was seeking a partner. Misty May and Kerri Walsh? The name sounded golden.

Smiling for Photographers
Albert L. Ortega / PR Photos

"Not being perfect makes the journey more fun."
- Kerri

Nicknamed *Six Feet of Sunshine*, Kerri Lee Walsh illuminated her parents' lives when she was born on August 15, 1978. Boasting blond curls and big blue eyes, the newest Walsh captured the heart of practically every person she met.

Kerri didn't speak much during the first few years of her life. In fact, the painfully shy, little girl often let her older brother, Marte, speak for her.

Kerri's parents, Margery Lee and Timothy Joseph Walsh, were accomplished athletes in their own right. Margery won Most Valuable Player in volleyball twice at Santa Clara University, and Timothy played minor league baseball, reaching AAA status with the Oakland A's.

Athletic talent extended outside the Walsh's immediate family, too. Kerri's paternal grandfather, Red, pitched for the now defunct San Francisco Seals, a minor league team in the Pacific Coast League. Meanwhile, Aunt Maureen remains the all-time leading basketball scorer at Pepperdine University.

For the first few years of Kerri's life, the Walsh family lived in Scotts Valley, California. The small city is located six miles from picturesque Monterey Bay. The blond hair, blue-eyed beauty grew up with three siblings: Marte and two younger sisters, Kelli and KC.

Marte was just eleven months older than Kerri, and she worshipped him. For much of her childhood, the little sister followed her big brother everywhere and emulated whatever he did.

When Marte asked to play baseball, Kerri signed up for the league, too. The San Francisco Giants fan wasn't bothered that she was the only girl playing in the league. She loved playing the sport, made the All-Star team, and carried high expectations for herself.

"I thought I'd become the first woman in the major leagues," Kerri later told the *San Francisco Chronicle*.

Later, Marte became obsessed with basketball, and Kerri quickly gained a strong appreciation for it, too. She played the sport for many years and harbored dreams of playing in the NBA.

When Kerri was eight months old, the Mays experienced a family tragedy. Kerri's baby brother died at only three months of age.

A Quiet Moment
Daniel Locke / PR Photos

Signing for a Cause
© PRN / PR Photos

"That changed me forever, and I don't think I realized it at the time," she later told *ESPN*.

Before Kerri began high school, the Walsh family moved to San Jose, the third largest city in California. The teenager became a Lion when she enrolled at Archbishop Mitty High School, a private Catholic school in San Jose located on 24 acres. It was at that school where Kerri would form her Olympic dreams and even compete against a fellow volleyball player named Misty May.

Kerri was pleased to learn that Archbishop Mitty High School offered a rich variety of clubs and sports. This prompted the teenager to join the volleyball and basketball teams.

A natural athlete, Kerri led her school's volleyball team to three state championships from 1993 to 1995. Her efforts earned her Gatorade's inaugural National High School Volleyball Player of the Year award in 1996. Interestingly enough, during high school, Kerri competed against future partner Misty May. After the game ended, Kerri wanted Misty's autograph on a towel, but she was too shy to approach her, so a friend asked for her. When Misty walked over to deliver the signed item, Kerri felt so shy that she ran away!

Volleyball wasn't the only sport Kerri excelled at. In 1995, the statuesque athlete also led her school's basketball team to a state championship. Who knows? Had the blonde eschewed her volleyball dreams, we might have seen her play in the WNBA, a professional basketball league in the United States.

Yet, volleyball remained Kerri's first love. She loved the team sport more than any other physical game in the world. During her senior year of high school, the prestigious Stanford University offered her a volleyball scholarship, and the thrilled athlete happily accepted it.

Kerri's volleyball career flourished at the esteemed college in Mountain View, California. She was selected as a first-team All-American four years in a row. The talented athlete was only the second player in college history to earn such a distinction.

Under Kerri's leadership, the Stanford Cardinals won more than 90% of their matches and recorded 122-victories in 133 matches. The team also notched four Pac-10 titles and won the NCAA Final Four title in 1996 and 1997. Kerri also took MVP honors in 1996.

Kerri graduated from Stanford in 2000 with a B.A. in American Studies. The determined athlete felt excited to pursue a professional career and hoped to compete at the Olympics one day. After all, her family's motto was always, "If you love something, go for it with all your heart."

All Glammed Up
© Glenn Harris / PR Photos

*"Respect needs to
be the foundation
of any great relationship."*
- Kerri

Together, Misty May-Treanor and Kerri Walsh Jennings are considered the greatest beach volleyball team of all time. Winners of three consecutive Olympic gold medals in women's beach volleyball, the duo dominated the sport from 2003-2012.

In 2000, the Mays and Walshes traveled to Australia to watch their daughters compete at the Sydney Olympics. Misty competed in beach volleyball with Holly McPeak, and Kerri, who had recently made the national team, played on the indoor volleyball team. By chance, the two families met at the competition and instantly hit it off. It wasn't long before both sets of parents suggested that Misty and Kerri pair up as a beach volleyball team.

Following the Olympics, Misty ended her partnership with Holly. Although she respected the older player immensely, the young player felt they weren't the best fit for one another.

"I needed to take a step back and learn the game at a slower pace," Misty told the *St. Petersburg Times*. "I just wanted to slow down. I wanted to be able to make mistakes. You grow as a player making mistakes. You may not finish at the top, but eventually you get better. I wanted to grow with someone."

No Sand in Sight
Anthony G. Moore / PR Photos

Meanwhile, Kerri had just finished fourth in indoor volleyball with Team USA at the Sydney Olympics. Although she enjoyed playing indoors, the player was interested in trying the beach version of the sport.

At their parents' suggestion Misty and Kerri began working as a team later that year. They weren't initially a perfect fit, but the team trained tirelessly to move as one. In addition, Kerri worked hard at fine-tuning her footwork in the sand which is different than playing on indoor volleyball's steady floor.

Throughout her transformation, Kerri practiced as much patience as she could muster. The complicated transition was a difficult one. It would take time and hard work to convert to a new type of volleyball game. The determined athlete asked as many questions as possible, absorbing every answer she was given.

"I looked like an idiot at first, I really did," Walsh told the *San Francisco Chronicle*. "I was embarrassed to practice in front of other people."

"I was kind of looking over my shoulder, figuring Misty was going to pick up someone else, and that would be understandable, but she decided to stick with me. I'm very fortunate."

During their partnership's first two years, Misty and Kerri kept expectations low as they adjusted to one another. At times, the women felt extremely frustrated by their adjustment period. However, both women sensed they were on the cusp of greatness, so they remained patient and continued working hard. Their perseverance would pay off in gold.

By 2003, Misty and Kerri began clicking as a team. The duo went undefeated the entire season culminating with an emotional victory at the world championships.

In most years, Misty and Kerri's unbeaten record would have made them heavy gold-medal favorites at the 2004 Athens Olympics. However, Misty was battling an abdominal injury, and some doubted she would recover in time.

Two months before the Olympics, Misty nursed the injury by wearing a corset or tape. Afterward, she underwent rehab while practicing furiously for the games. Anyone who underestimated Misty's determination had never met her.

When Misty and Kerri finally arrived in Athens, they felt determined to play their best. The team silenced any doubters right away, performing fluidly in early rounds by defeating teams from Japan, Netherlands, and Czech Republic.

On August 23, two American teams squared off in the quarter-finals. Misty and Kerri faced Holly McPeak and Elaine Youngs. In the end, youth prevailed over experience. Misty and Kerri won the showdown and headed to the finals to play for the gold medal!

The mood was festive at Faliro Beach Volleyball Stadium for the gold medal battle. Misty and Kerri would face Brazil's Adriana Behar and Shelda Bede for top honors. The winners would call themselves Olympic champions for the rest of their lives.

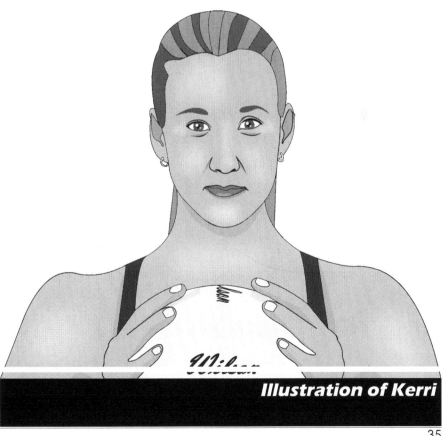

Illustration of Kerri

In the end, the competition was never close. Misty and Kerri were dominant, winning the gold in just 43 minutes. When the women's Olympic beach volleyball competition ended, the top Americans never lost a set throughout the entire competition.

Upon realizing they won gold, the two women embraced for a long time. The crowd cheered loudly for their impressive victory. When Kerri spotted her brother in the stands, she ran to hug him. Later at the medal ceremony, both women grinned widely as the American flag was raised while the national anthem played proudly in the background.

"We didn't play the prettiest volleyball, but we adjusted and played great defense," a modest Kerri analyzed.

Misty and Kerri were the world's best volleyball players, and now they had the gold medal to prove it. Still such a young team, it was entirely conceivable to imagine they would return for another Olympics, or even two.

Teamwork
Daniel Locke / PR Photos

"Experience in Beach Volleyball comes into play in those big matches where fatigue sets in."
- Misty

Following the Athens Games, the new Olympic champions continued ruling beach volleyball. Displaying even greater confidence than ever, the dynamic duo captured world titles in 2005 and 2007.

Before they knew it, another Olympics had arrived. Beijing, China, hosted the 2008 Summer Games. Needless to say, Misty and Kerri were the overwhelming favorites to win the gold medal among the 24 pairs entered. Furthermore, the pair had the opportunity to accomplish what no women's beach volleyball team had done: win back-to-back Olympic titles.

Shortly before the Opening Ceremonies, Misty and Kerri received a thrilling visit from President George W. Bush. The Commander-in-Chief visited with the American superstars giving them a pep talk.

"Show me something out there," President Bush urged them.

"We'll make you proud," Kerri vowed.

After breezy victories in their early matches, Misty and Kerri would face China's Tian Jia and Wang Jie in the gold medal match. It rained on Beach Volleyball

Ground at Chaoyang Park on the big day but wet weather wouldn't prevent the match from happening. History was at stake.

Twelve thousand screaming fans arrived to cheer on home country players Tian Jia and Wang Jie. If Misty and Kerri wanted to win a second straight title, they would have to block out the intense support for their rivals. Kerri silently pretended the crowd was actually cheering for her and Misty.

The gold medal showdown lived up to the hype. Both teams played superbly with a tie score 12 times in the first match. In the end, though, the Americans' experience, camaraderie, and technical skills propelled them to a second Olympic title. Following the competition, Misty was named Most Outstanding Player for the women's event.

"The rain makes it better," Kerri gushed afterward. "We felt like warriors out there. The pressure of playing China made it pretty intense."

"The Chinese team is amazing," Misty gushed. "They are so young and they pressed us so hard in the match. I feel proud to play with them in the final."

After the match ended, Misty and Kerri showed why many consider them great role models. The thoughtful duo thanked all the volunteers for their hard work, even chasing down some people before they left.

Following their gold medal win at the Beijing Olympics, Misty and Kerri competed at the 2008 AVP Crocs Cup Shootout. It was at that competition where their 112 straight match victory streak ended after an upset victory by Olympic teammates Nicole Branagh and Elaine Youngs.

In autumn of 2008, Misty stepped away from volleyball to appear on ABC's reality competition series *Dancing with the Stars*. Teamed with Maksim Chmerkovskiy, she was predicted to excel on the show. Sadly, a few weeks into filming, the volleyball player ruptured her Achilles tendon during dance practice. Needing surgery, she withdrew from the competition.

"I'm really bummed," Misty told *PEOPLE* magazine. "We don't know why these things happen. They could happen to anyone. I feel like I was only just beginning here."

Meanwhile, Kerri kept busy herself. Married to pro volleyball player Casey Jennings since December 2005, the couple became parents on May 22, 2009, when they welcomed their first child, Joseph Michael. Eleven months later, they added another child to their family with the birth of a second son, Sundance Thomas.

Misty's personal life also flourished off the sand. In early 2004, she began dating baseball player Matt Treanor. The pair turned serious very quickly and they were married in November of 2004. The two often talked of starting a family when Misty's career eventually ended.

A professional athlete himself, Matt understood the time, sacrifice, and dedication that a sports career demanded. The tall, handsome catcher played for many Major League Baseball teams throughout his lengthy career, including the Los Angeles Dodgers, Florida Marlins, Detroit Tigers, and Texas Rangers.

By 2011, Misty and Kerri had taken almost a year off from volleyball. Both felt anxious to return to their beloved sport. They felt strong, ready, and determined to compete again.

Meanwhile, the London Olympics was right around the corner. Could Misty May-Treanor and Kerri Walsh Jennings make it a three-peat?

Golden Girls
Scott Alan / PR Photos

"For me to be able to play with (Misty) so long and be able to call her a friend and a sister is the biggest gift ever."
- Kerri

Misty May-Treanor declared months before the start of the London Olympics that the competition would mark the final one of her career. She was ready to retire. The volleyball legend felt excited to start a family with her husband.

"There's more to life than volleyball," she told *Vollywood.net*. "It's time for me to step away."

At the 2012 Summer Olympic Games, Misty and Kerri began strongly by notching several victories. They soundly defeated Australia, Czech Republic, Austria, Netherlands, Italy, and China.

Ultimately, the gold medal showdown came down to two American teams. The reigning champions would battle Jennifer Kessy and April Ross for gold. All four women trained in Southern California.

In the end, Misty and Kerri created a fairy tale ending to their beach volleyball partnership. They handily won the final 2-0 (21-16, 21-16). The duo had taken their third consecutive Olympic gold medal in beach volleyball.

Upon realizing they had won an unprecedented third title, Misty pumped her fists triumphantly, while

Kerri jumped jubilantly into the air. After a long embrace, the volleyball stars ran to the stands to celebrate the historic achievement with loved ones.

In the midst of baseball season, Matt Treanor was unable to travel to London. He watched the match on a laptop at Dodger Stadium in the trainer's room. Misty's husband became quite emotional when discussing the team's victory.

"It was tears of joy," Matt told *MLB.com*. "Honestly, the tears didn't flow right away, because there were people in the room. I had to step out.

"It's a swarming effect. There are all these thoughts and emotions that come in your head, and it's just about Misty and what she wanted to do."

Following their remarkable third victory, Misty and Kerri were in high demand after London. They gave interviews to television, print, radio, and internet reporters. Throughout their appearances Misty confirmed her desire to retire, while Kerri reiterated her plan to stay in the sport by finding a new partner.

Despite ending their competitive partnership, Misty and Kerri's friendship would remain dear friends. The two had formed a strong bond and vowed to remain a constant presence in each other's lives.

"I will never leave her side," Misty vowed.

Casey and Kerri
Izumi Hasegawa / PR Photos

*"To see where girls'
athletics have come is
fantastic. Women were
really prominent in (the
2012) Olympic games. I
think it's our time."*
- Misty

Made in the USA
Monee, IL
09 November 2020

47106712R00028